THE BOOK OF OBADIAH BIBLE STUDY GUIDE

Common People Series

Paula Land

THE PURPOSE OF THIS GUIDE

Mark 12:37...And the common people heard him gladly

The twelfth chapter of Mark begins with Jesus teaching a parable and as usual, the Pharisees, Sadducees and scribes began to flaunt their scholarly knowledge and tried to snare Him in His own words. In the background, is a group of special people mentioned. They were the common people.... **And the common people heard him gladly.**

As in Biblical times, the common people are not less intelligent but many do lack confidence and encouragement to read the Word of God. The lack of confidence in our ability to read and learn the scriptures discourages us from actually reading them. What seems as a lack of confidence in ourselves, however, is wrongly placed false humility. It is our lack of FAITH in the Holy Spirit to teach us to skillfully handle the Word of God.

This guide includes general Bible knowledge and deeper studies . But it's intent is not just to impart knowledge. Ultimately, it is to help you increase your faith in the Holy Spirit that He **will** guide and teach **you** to skillfully handle the Word of God. You may at first follow this guide to the letter. But it won't be long before you are allowing the Holy Spirit to lead you through your own reading.
John 16:13 Howbeit when he, the Spirit of truth, is come, he will guide you into all truth: for he shall not speak of himself; but whatsoever he shall hear, that shall he speak.

The Bible is the inspired Word of God and consists of 66 books. You can follow this inspiration from one book of the Bible to the next by looking for shadows, patterns, similiarities and cross references. I have included my own studies to help you learn how to recognize some of these.

HOW TO USE THIS GUIDE

1. **You must use the King James Bible.** All answers correspond to the King James Bible.

2. The chapters are divided into sections. Each section has two pages. The lower page is for you to fill in the blanks and record your own notes. The opposite page is a duplicate and is titled KEY with the answers written in *script*. I have intentionally used pictures that are black and white, faceless, and unremarkable to avoid preconceived notions and ideas.

3. The opposite page (KEY) has the completed answers written in *script*. Also written in *script* are my notes. Some of these notes are as simple as definitions of words or phrases that may be unfamiliar and possibly hinder the understanding. Others are deep Bible studies that leaves us in awe of God's Word.

4. This is important. Answer each question in numerical order because they are numbered according to the sequence of events. Some pages contain a lot of information and are very busy. Each question already has the first letter already completed so you don't lose your thoughts trying to figure out what is being asked.

5. Don't try to study outside sources to clarify the meaning. There is no historical or archaeological information from antiquities or Greek/Hebrew lexicons included. This is not necessary because the King James Bible is plenary meaning complete. If you want to do a deeper study, search the Bible for similar verses, phrases or ideas. These can be easily found by using a concordance (a book that lists words of the Bible in alphabetical order). The Webster's 1828 Dictionary is an excellent source to find definitions to biblical words that may have dropped out of today's vocabulary.

6. Maps are used for general locations only. They are not exactly to scale but serve to keep places and events in context.

The Book of Obadiah

Background

The only background we need is provided for us throughout the Bible. We don't need archaelogical evidence, antiquities or whatever. Trust the Bible to be complete in itself. To help gain confidence in the Bible, try to find these facts as your are reading through it.

The book of Obadiah is the shortest book of the Bible but contains some dire warnings to the nations. God uses Jacob and Esau and their struggle from the womb as a prophecy to the heathen nations of the world and the millenial kingdom. Esau is the father of the Edomites while Jacob, his twin brother, is the father of the Israelites. Edom is located slightly southwest of Israel and is a heathen nation. They aided the enemies of the Israelites when they were taken into captivity and God has judged them for their betrayal. The book concludes with a warning to all heathen nations and the prosperity of Israel, God's chosen people.

Read Obadiah

Matthew 5:18 For verily I say unto you, Till heaven and earth pass, one jot or one tittle shall in no wise pass from the law, till all be fulfilled.

V.1 A
GUIDE

① V.1 The vision
of *Obadiah.*

Thus saith the *Lord GOD* concerning...

② V. 1 ...*Edom;*

ARAM

PHOENICIA

ISRAEL

AMMON

Dead
Sea

MOAB

JUDAH

IDUMEA

PHILISTIA

EDOM

Gulf of
Aqaba

0 20 50 km

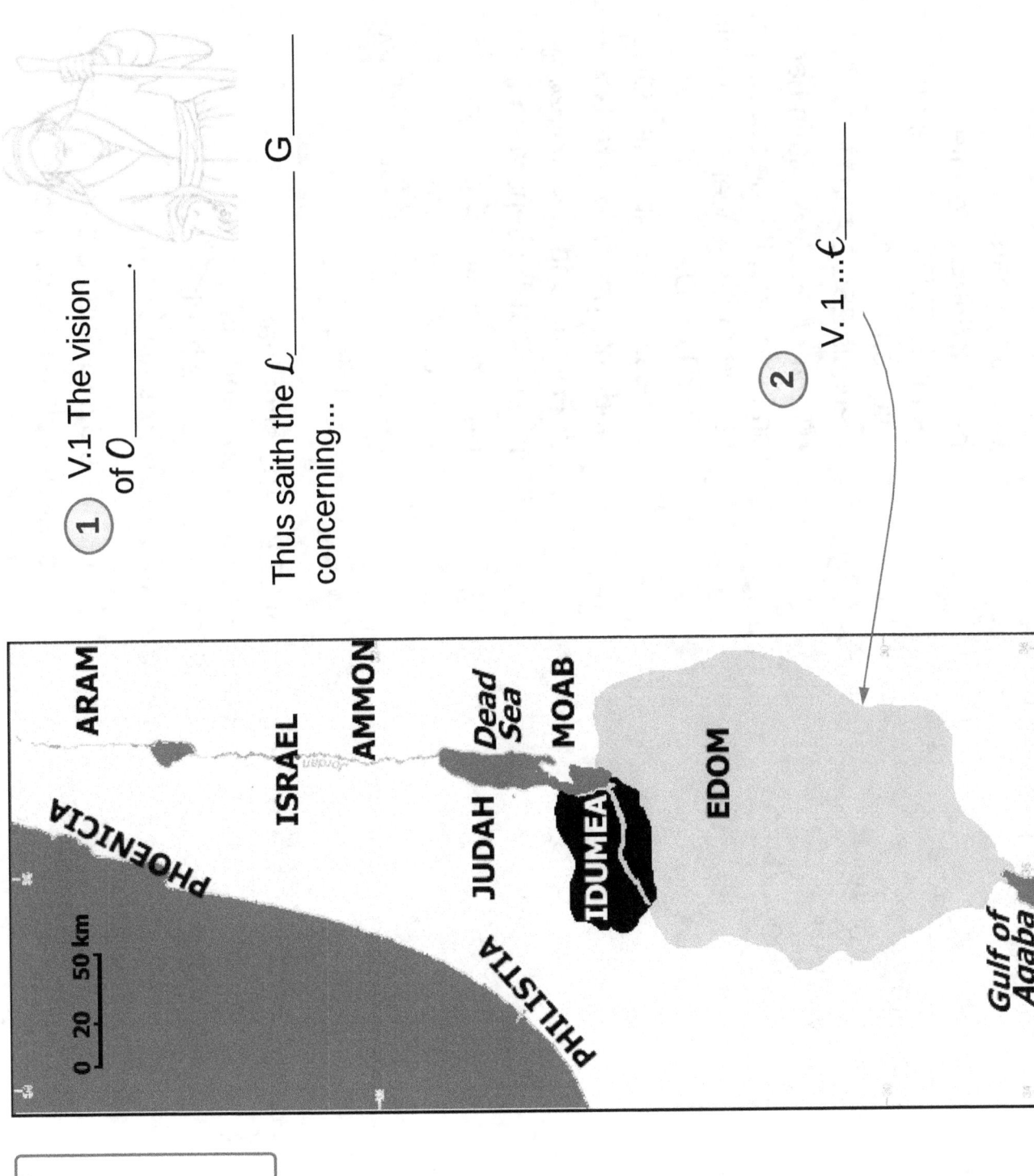

V.1 A NOTES

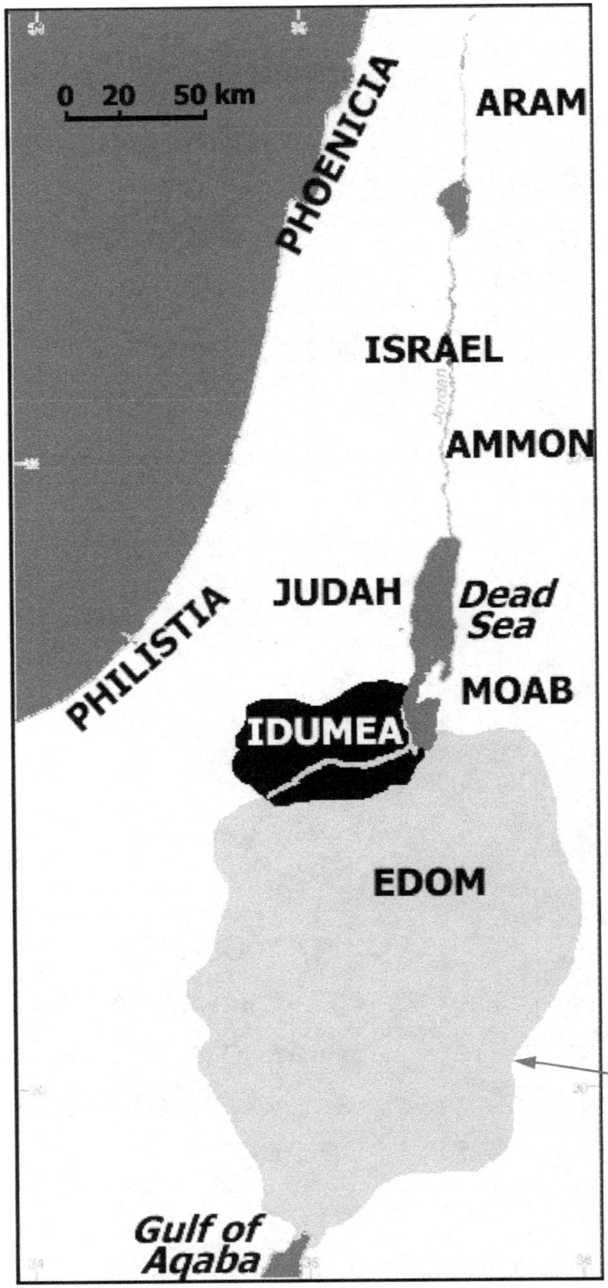
0 20 50 km
PHOENICIA
ARAM
ISRAEL
AMMON
JUDAH
Dead Sea
PHILISTIA
MOAB
IDUMEA
EDOM
Gulf of Aqaba

1. V.1 The vision of *O*__________.

Thus saith the *L*__________ G______ concerning...

2. V. 1 ...*E*______

Edom
GUIDE

② Genesis 25:19 And these are the generations of Isaac, Abraham's son: Abraham begat Isaac:

Abraham

① *Isaac*

③ *Rebekah*

Genesis 25:20 And Isaac was forty years old when he took *Rebekah* to wife,

Genesis 25:21... Rebekah his wife conceived.

Genesis 25:22 *And the children struggled together within her;* and she said, If it be so, why am I thus? And she went to enquire of the LORD.

Genesis 25:23 And the LORD said unto her, *Two nations are in thy womb, and two manner of people shall be separated from thy bowels; and the one people shall be stronger than the other people; and the elder shall serve the younger.*

opposite →

④ Genesis 25:25 *And the first came out red, all over like an hairy garment; and they called his name Esau.*

⑤ Genesis 25:26 And after that came his brother out, and his hand took hold on Esau's heel; *and his name was called Jacob:*

⑦ Genesis 32:28 And he said, Thy name shall be called *no more Jacob, but Israel:*

⑥ Genesis 36:8-9 Thus dwelt Esau in mount Seir: <u>Esau is Edom.</u> And these are the generations of *Esau the father of the Edomites in mount Seir:*

ARAM
PHOENICIA
ISRAEL
AMMON
Dead Sea
JUDAH
MOAB
PHILISTIA
IDUMEA
EDOM
Mt. Seir
Gulf of Aqaba
0 20 50 km

Edom
NOTES

2

A _____

Genesis 25:19 And these are the generations of Isaac, Abraham's son: Abraham begat Isaac:

I _____

3

Genesis 25:20 And Isaac was forty years old when he took _____ to wife,

R _____

Genesis 25:21... Rebekah his wife conceived.

S _____

Genesis 25:22 And the children _____ together within her; and she said, If it be so, why am I thus? And she went to enquire of the LORD.

Genesis 25:23 And the LORD said unto her, T_____ n_____ *are* (opposite) in thy w_____, and t_____ m_____ of p_____ shall be separated from thy bowels; and the one people shall be s_____ than the other people; and the e_____ shall s_____ the y_____.

1 Rebekah

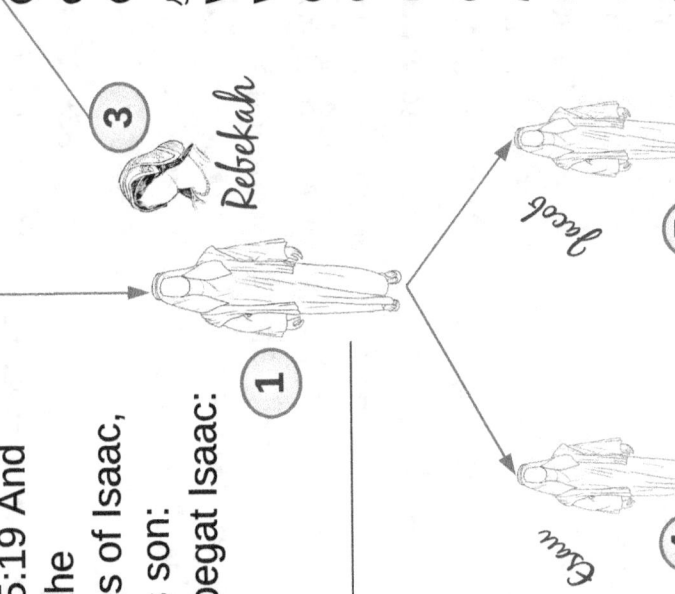

5 Jacob

4

Genesis 25:25 And the f_____ came out red, all over like an hairy garment; and they called his name E_____.

6

Map labels: ARAM, PHOENICIA, ISRAEL, AMMON, Dead Sea, MOAB, JUDAH, IDUMEA, EDOM, Mt. Seir, PHILISTIA, Gulf of Aqaba — 0 20 50 km

Genesis 36:8-9 Thus dwelt Esau in mount Seir: Esau is Edom. And these are the generations of Esau the f_____ of the E_____ in m_____ S_____:

7

Genesis 25:26 And after that came his brother out, and his hand took hold on Esau's heel; and his name was called J_____.

Genesis 32:28 And he said, Thy name shall be called n_____ m_____ J_____, but I_____:

Two Manners of Esau and Jacob

The Two Manners of Esau and Jacob

Esau (Edom)   Jacob (Israel)

Genesis 25:27-34 And the boys grew: and Esau was a cunning hunter, a man of the field; and Jacob was a plain man, dwelling in tents. And Isaac loved Esau, because he did eat of his venison: but Rebekah loved Jacob. And Jacob sod pottage: and Esau came from the field, and he was faint: And Esau said to Jacob, Feed me, I pray thee, with that same red pottage; for I am faint: therefore was his name called Edom. And Jacob said, Sell me this day thy birthright. And Esau said, Behold, I am at the point to die: and what profit shall this birthright do to me? And Jacob said, Swear to me this day; and he sware unto him: and he sold his birthright unto Jacob. Then Jacob gave Esau bread and pottage of lentiles; and he did eat and drink, and rose up, and went his way: thus Esau despised his birthright.

Hebrews 12:16 Lest there be any fornicator, or profane person, as Esau, who for one morsel of meat sold his birthright.

Hebrews 12:17 For ye know how that afterward, when he would have inherited the blessing, he was rejected: for he found no place of repentance, though he sought it carefully with tears.

no repentance for physical things

Genesis 32:23-30 And he took them, and sent them over the brook, and sent over that he had. And Jacob was left alone; and there wrestled a man with him until the breaking of the day. And when he saw that he prevailed not against him, he touched the hollow of his thigh; and the hollow of Jacob's thigh was out of joint, as he wrestled with him. And he said, Let me go, for the day breaketh. And he said, I will not let thee go, except thou bless me. And he said unto him, What is thy name? And he said, Jacob. And he said, Thy name shall be called no more Jacob, but Israel: for as a prince hast thou power with God and with men, and hast prevailed. And Jacob asked him, and said, Tell me, I pray thee, thy name. And he said, Wherefore is it that thou dost ask after my name? And he blessed him there. And Jacob called the name of the place Peniel: for I have seen God face to face, and my life is preserved.

Esau wanted to please the flesh. Jacob was willing to fight for a spiritual blessing.

Two Manners of Esau and Jacob

NOTES

The Two Manners of Esau and Jacob

 Esau (Edom)

Jacob (Israel)

Genesis 25:27-34 And the boys grew: and E_____ was a cunning h_____, a man of the field; and J_____ was a plain man, dwelling in t_____. And I_____ loved E_____, because he did eat of his venison: but R_____ loved J_____. And Jacob sod pottage: and Esau came from the field, and he was faint: And Esau said to Jacob, F_____ me, I pray thee, with that same r_____ pottage; for I am faint: therefore was his name called Edom. And Jacob said, S_____ me this day t_____ b_____. And Esau said, Behold, I am at the point to die: and what profit shall this birthright do to me? And Jacob said, Swear to me this day; and he sware unto him: and he s_____ his b_____ unto J_____. Then Jacob gave Esau bread and pottage of lentiles; and he did eat and drink, and rose up, and went his way: thus E_____ d_____ his b_____.

Genesis 32:23-30 And he took them, and sent them over the brook, and sent over that he had. And J_____ was left alone; and there w_____ a man with him until the breaking of the day. And when he saw that he prevailed not against him, he touched the h_____ of his t_____; and the hollow of Jacob's thigh was out of j_____, as he wrestled with him. And he said, Let me go, for the day breaketh. And he said, I will not let thee go, e_____ thou b_____ m_____. And he said unto him, What is thy name? And he said, Jacob. And he said, Thy name shall be called no more J_____, but I_____: for as a p_____ hast thou w_____ and with G_____ and hast prevailed. And Jacob asked m_____, and said, Tell me, I pray thee, thy name. And he said, Wherefore is it that thou dost ask after my name? And h_____ b_____ h_____ t_____. And Jacob called the name of the place Peniel: for I have seen God face to face, and my life is preserved.

CONCERNING EDOM

V.1-4 GUIDE

The vision of Obadiah.
Thus saith the Lord GOD concerning Edom

(1) V. 1...We have heard a rumour from the LORD, and an ambassador is sent among *the heathen,* Arise ye, and let us rise up against her in battle.

V.2 Behold, *I have made thee small among the* heathen: *thou art greatly despised.*

gentiles– anyone not of the Jews. Edom was heathen.

NIV completely omits the word Lucifer in the entire version. It never teaches Lucifer is Satan!

V.3 The **pride of thine heart** hath deceived thee, thou that dwellest in the (2) *clefts of the rock,* whose habitation is high; that (4) *saith in his heart,* Who shall (6) *bring me down to the ground?*

USA?   *flag?*

V.4 Though **thou exalt thyself** (8) *as the eagle,* and though thou set thy nest (10) *among the stars,* thence will (12) *I bring thee down,* saith the LORD.

Edom exalted himself as Satan exalted himself and was cast down from heaven.

thou exalt thyself....I Will
Pride of thine heart

Edom ← ← Lucifer

Isaiah 14:12 How art thou fallen from heaven, O *Lucifer,* son of the morning! how art thou (7) *cut down to the ground,* which didst weaken the nations!

Isaiah 14:13 For thou (5) *hast said in thine heart,* **I will** ascend into heaven, **I will** exalt my throne (11) *above the stars* of God: **I will sit** also (3) *upon the mount* of the congregation, in the sides of the north:

Isaiah 14:14 **I will** ascend above the heights of the clouds; **I will** (9) *be like the most High.*

Isaiah 14:15 Yet (13) *thou shalt be brought down* to hell, to the sides of the pit.

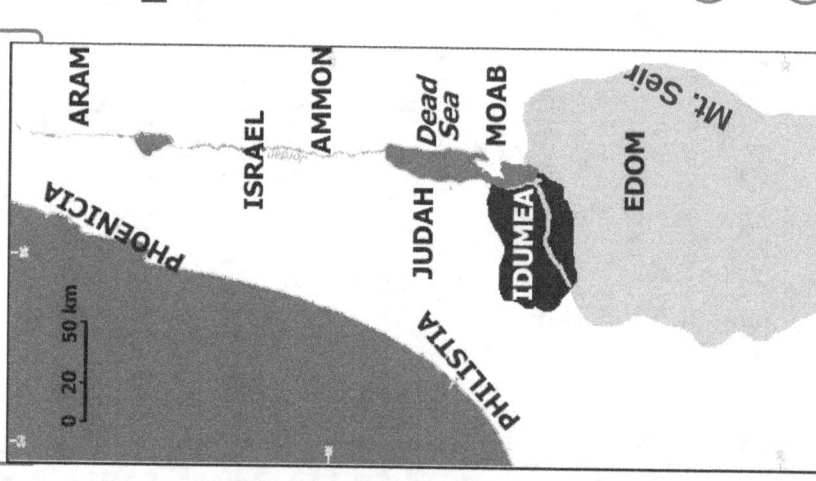

ARAM
ISRAEL
AMMON
PHOENICIA
JUDAH
Dead Sea
MOAB
IDUMEA
Mt. Seir
EDOM
PHILISTIA
Gulf of Aqaba
0 20 50 km

CONCERNING EDOM

The vision of Obadiah.
Thus saith the Lord GOD concerning Edom

(1) V. 1…We have heard a rumour from the LORD, and an a_____ is sent a_the_ h_____, Arise ye, and let us rise up against her in battle.

V.2 Behold, _I have made thee_ s_____ _d_ among the heathen: thou art g_____.

V.3 The **pride of thine heart** hath deceived thee, thou that dwellest in the (2) c_____ of the r_____, whose habitation is h_____; that (4) s_____ in his h_____, (6) b_____ me d_____ ?

V.4 Though **thou exalt thyself** (8) _as the e_, and though thou set thy nest (10) _among the_ s_____, thence will _I_ (12) b_____ _t_ d_____, saith the LORD.

thou exalt thyself….I Will
Pride of thine heart

Isaiah 14:12 How art thou fallen from heaven, (3) O _L_____, son _cut_ of the morning! how art thou (9) _d_____ to the g_____, which didst weaken the nations!

Isaiah 14:13 For thou (5) _hast_ said in thine h_____ s_____, **I will** ascend into heaven, **I will** exalt my throne (11) _above the s_____ of God: **I will sit** also (3) _upon the m_____ of the congregation, in the sides of the north:

Isaiah 14:14 **I will** ascend above the heights of the clouds; **I will** (9) _be_ _the m_____ H_____.

Isaiah 14:15 Yet (13) _thou shalt be_ b_____ d_____ to hell, to the sides of the pit.

V.1-4 NOTES

CONCERNING EDOM

The vision of Obadiah.
Thus saith the Lord GOD concerning Edom

Luke 12:33 Sell that ye have, and give alms; provide yourselves bags which wax not old, a treasure in the heavens that faileth not, where no thief approacheth, neither moth corrupteth.

Jesus will come like a thief in the night.

V.5 If thieves came to thee, if *robbers by night,* (how art thou cut off!) would they not have stolen till they had enough?

Angels

if the grapegatherers came to thee, would they not leave some grapes? (No! God always leaves a remnant of His people but he will utterly destroy the Edomites.)

Grape harvest is the last of the Jewish Feasts. It is symbolic of the end of the world judgment.

Revelation 14:19 And the angel thrust in his sickle into the earth, and gathered the vine of the earth, and cast it into the great winepress of the wrath of God.

Revelation 14:20 And the winepress was trodden without the city, and blood came out of the winepress, even unto the horse bridles, by the space of a thousand and six hundred furlongs.

winepress represents the wrath of God

Juice from the grapes is blood of men.

Prophecy that has already been fulfilled. Edom no longer exists as a nation.

Isaiah 63:1 Who is this that cometh from *Edom,* with dyed garments from Bozrah? this that is glorious in his apparel, travelling in the greatness of his strength? I that speak in righteousness, mighty to save.

Trying to like Christ in glorious white apparel

stained from grapes/blood

Isaiah 63:2 Wherefore art thou *red* in thine apparel, and thy garments like him that *treadeth* in the winefat?

Isaiah 63:3 I have trodden the *winepress* alone; and of the people there was none with me: for I will tread them in mine anger, and trample them in my fury; and *their blood* shall be sprinkled upon my garments, and I will *stain* all my raiment.

with the blood of Edom

Isaiah 63:4 For the day of vengeance is in mine heart, and the year of my redeemed is come.

the day God executed judgment

God's people and land

V.5 GUIDE

The vision of Obadiah.
Thus saith the Lord GOD
concerning Edom

CONCERNING EDOM

V.5 If t_____ came to thee, if r_____ by _____, (how art thou cut off!) would they not have stolen till they had enough?

if the g_____ came to thee, would they not leave some g_____?

Isaiah 63:1 Who is this that cometh from E_____, with dyed garments from Bozrah? this that is g_____ in his apparel, travelling in the greatness of his strength? I that speak in righteousness, mighty to save.

Isaiah 63:2 Wherefore art thou r_____ in thine apparel, and thy garments like him that t_____ in the w_____?

Isaiah 63:3 I have trodden the w_____ alone; and of the people there was none with me: for I will tread them in mine anger, and trample them in my fury; and their b_____ shall be sprinkled upon my garments, and I will s_____ all my raiment.

Isaiah 63:4 For the day of V_____ is in mine heart, and the year of my r_____ is come.

V.5 NOTES

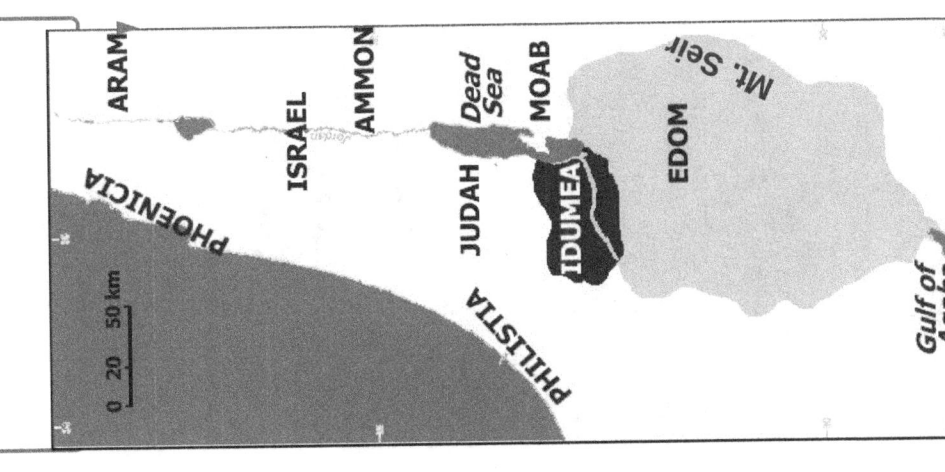

ARAM
AMMON
ISRAEL
Dead Sea
MOAB
JUDAH
IDUMEA
Mt. Seir
EDOM
PHOENICIA
PHILISTIA
Gulf of Aqaba
0 20 50 km

CONCERNING EDOM

The vision of Obadiah.
Thus saith the Lord GOD concerning Edom

Malachi 1:2 I have loved you, saith the LORD. Yet ye say, Wherein hast thou loved us? Was not Esau Jacob's brother? saith the LORD: yet I loved Jacob,
Malachi 1:3 And I hated Esau, and laid his mountains and his heritage waste for the dragons of the wilderness.

Edom

V.6 How are the things of *Esau* searched out! how are his *hidden things* sought up!

God knew what manner of pride Esau had when he was still in the womb. Eventually Esau's pride was revealed.

V.6 GUIDE

0 20   50 km

PHOENICIA
ARAM
ISRAEL
AMMON
JUDAH
Dead Sea
IDUMEA
MOAB
EDOM
Mt. Seir
Petra
Gulf of Aqaba
PHILISTIA

The vision of Obadiah.
Thus saith the Lord GOD
concerning Edom

CONCERNING EDOM

V.6
NOTES

V.6 How are the things of E_____
searched out! how are his
h_____
sought up!

Petra

ARAM

ISRAEL

AMMON

Dead
Sea

MOAB

JUDAH

IDUMEA

Mt. Seir

EDOM

PHOENICIA

PHILISTIA

Gulf of
Aqaba

0 20 50 km

CONCERNING EDOM

**The vision of Obadiah.
Thus saith the Lord GOD
concerning Edom**

*a league or covenant,
mutual agreement*

V.7 All the men of thy confederacy have brought thee even to the border: the men that were at peace with thee have *deceived* thee, and *prevailed* against thee; that they eat *thy bread* have laid *a wound* under thee: there is *none understanding* in him.

traitors

V.8 Shall I not in that day, saith the LORD, even destroy *the wise men* out of Edom, and *understanding* out of the *mount of Esau?*

V.9 And thy mighty men, O *Teman*, shall be dismayed, to the end that every one of the *mount of Esau* may be cut off by *slaughter.*

Genesis 36:10 These are the names of Esau's sons; <u>Eliphaz</u> the son of Adah the wife of Esau, Reuel the son of Bashemath the wife of Esau.
Genesis 36:11 And the sons of Eliphaz were <u>Teman</u>, Omar, Zepho, and Gatam, and Kenaz.

Teman was Esau's eldest Grandson Text

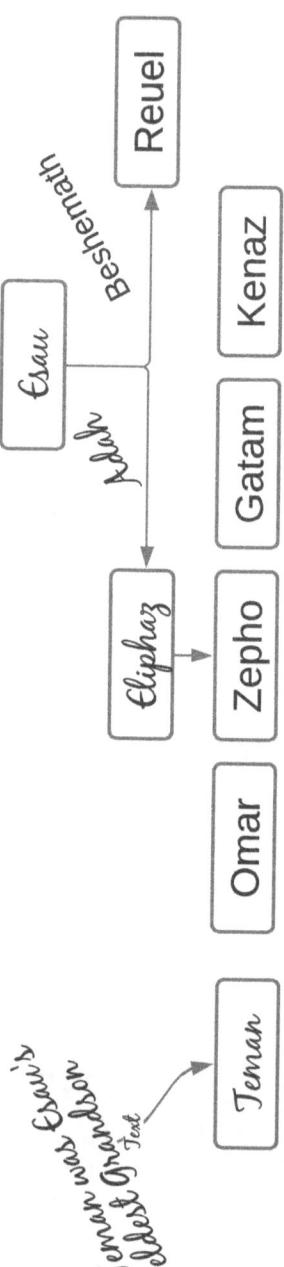

Esau
Adah — Beshemath
Eliphaz — Reuel
Teman   Omar   Zepho   Gatam   Kenaz

V.7-9
GUIDE

[Map showing:]
ARAM
PHOENICIA
ISRAEL
AMMON
Dead Sea
JUDAH
IDUMEA
MOAB
PHILISTIA
EDOM
Mt. Seir
Teman
Gulf of Aqaba
0 20 50 km

CONCERNING EDOM

The vision of Obadiah.
Thus saith the Lord GOD
concerning Edom

V.7 All the men of thy c_____ have brought thee
even to the border: the men that were at p_____ with thee have
d_____ thee, and p_____ against thee; that they
eat *thy b*_____ have laid *a w*_____ under thee: there
is *n*_____ *w*_____ in him.

V.8 Shall I not in that day, saith the LORD, even destroy *the w*_____
men out of Edom, and *u*_____ out of the *mount of*
*E*_____?

V.9 And thy mighty men, *O T*_____, shall be dismayed, to the
end that every one of the *mount of Esau* may be cut off by *s*_____ .

Genesis 36:10 These are the
names of Esau's sons; Eliphaz
the son of Adah the wife of
Esau, Reuel the son of
Bashemath the wife of Esau.
Genesis 36:11 And the sons of
Eliphaz were Teman, Omar,
Zepho, and Gatam, and Kenaz.

V.7-9
NOTES

(MAP) Valp, CC BY-SA 4.0 <https://creativecommons.org/licenses/by-sa/4.0>, via Wikimedia Commons

Reuel

Bashemath

Adah

E_____

E_____

Omar   Zepho   Gatam   Kenaz

T_____

The vision of Obadiah. Thus saith the Lord GOD concerning Edom

CONCERNING EDOM

Jacob and Esau struggled in the womb.

Genesis 25:22 And the children struggled together within her; and she said, If it be so, why am I thus? And she went to enquire of the LORD.

The Pride of Thine Heart

1 V.10 For thy *violence against thy brother Jacob*

2 V.10 ...*shame* shall cover thee

3 V.10 and thou shalt be *cut off for ever.*

Psalm 137:7 Remember, O LORD, the children of Edom in the day of Jerusalem; who said, *Rase it, rase it, even to the foundation thereof.*

the day of judgment for Jerusalem when they were carried away captive.

To erase; to scratch or rub out; or to blot out; to cancel.
They called for Jerusalem to blotted out. Even so, God did to them.

V.10 GUIDE

ARAM
PHOENICIA
ISRAEL
AMMON
JUDAH
Dead Sea
IDUMEA
MOAB
EDOM
Mt. Seir
PHILISTIA
Gulf of Aqaba

0 20 50 km

The vision of Obadiah. Thus saith the Lord GOD concerning Edom

CONCERNING EDOM

Genesis 25:22 And the children struggled together within her; and she said, If it be so, why am I thus? And she went to enquire of the LORD.

The Pride of Thine Heart

1 V.10 For thy v_____ _____ against thy brother J_____

2 V.10 ...s_____ shall cover thee

3 V.10 and thou shalt be c_____
b_____ e_____ off .

Psalm 137:7 Remember, O LORD, the children of Edom in the day of Jerusalem; who said, Rase it, rase it, even to the foundation thereof.

V.10
NOTES.

The vision of Obadiah. Thus saith the Lord GOD concerning Edom

CONCERNING EDOM

Genesis 25:22 And the children struggled together within her; and she said, If it be so, why am I thus? And she went to enquire of the LORD.

The Pride of Thine Heart

V.11 In the day that thou stoodest on the other side, in the day that the strangers carried away captive his forces, and foreigners entered into his gates, and cast lots upon Jerusalem,

even thou wast as one of them.

① V.12 But thou shouldest not have looked on the day of thy brother in the day that he became a stranger;

② V.12 ...neither shouldest thou have rejoiced over the children of Judah in the day of their destruction;

③ V.12 ...neither shouldest thou have spoken proudly in the day of distress.

Foreigner in a strange land

Tribe of the children of Israel from which Jesus came

(MAP) Valp, CC BY-SA 4.0 <https://creativecommons.org/licenses/by-sa/4.0>, via Wikimedia Commons

V.11-12 GUIDE

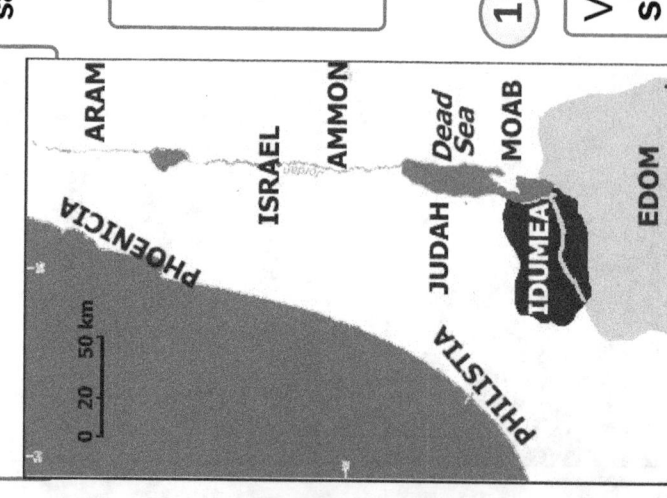

ARAM

PHOENICIA

ISRAEL

AMMON

JUDAH

Dead Sea

MOAB

IDUMEA

EDOM

Mt. Seir

PHILISTIA

Gulf of Aqaba

0   20   50 km

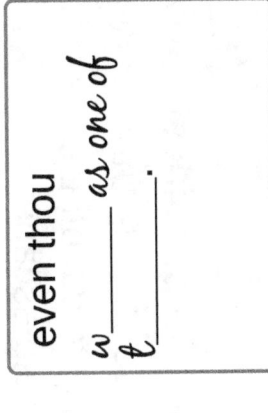

The vision of Obadiah. Thus saith the Lord GOD concerning Edom

CONCERNING EDOM

Genesis 25:22 And the children <u>struggled together within her;</u> and she said, If it be so, why am I thus? And she went to enquire of the LORD.

The Pride of Thine Heart

V.11 In the day that thou stoodest on the other side, <u>in the day that the strangers carried away captive his forces,</u> and foreigners entered into his gates, and cast lots upon Jerusalem,

even thou
w_____ as one of
t_____ .

③ V.12 ...neither shouldest thou have spoken p_____ in the d_____ of d_____ .

② V.12 ...neither shouldest thou have r_____ over the children of J_____ in the day of their d_____ ;

① V.12 But thou shouldest not have looked on the day of thy brother in the day that h_____ became a s_____ ;

V.11-12 NOTES

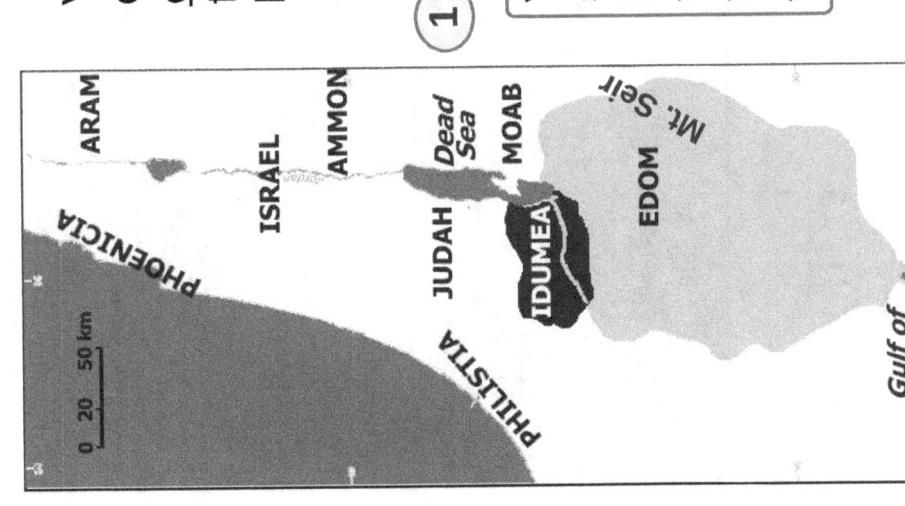

The vision of Obadiah. Thus saith
the Lord GOD concerning Edom

CONCERNING EDOM

**Genesis 25:22 And the <u>children struggled together</u> within her; and she
said, If it be so, why am I thus? And she went to enquire of the LORD.**

*Edom did not help their brother Israel when
they were attacked by Nebuchadnezzar
(Babylon) and taken captive.*

④ **V.13 Thou shouldest
not** have entered into the
gate of my people in the
day of their calamity;
yea,

⑤ **V. 13... thou shouldest not**
have looked on their affliction
in the day of their calamity,

*Stood by and
watched.*

⑥ **nor** have laid hands
on their substance in
the day of their
calamity; *looted*

⑦ **V.14 Neither shouldest
thou** have stood in the
crossway, to cut off those of
his that did escape;   *blocked
their
escape*

⑧ V. 14 neither shouldest thou
have delivered up those of his
that did remain in the day of
distress.

*They turned in those that
escaped the attack.*

V.13-14
GUIDE

(Map) Valp, CC BY-SA 4.0
<https://creativecommons.org/licenses/by-sa/4.0>, via Wikimedia
Commons

V.13-14 NOTES

CONCERNING EDOM

The vision of Obadiah. Thus saith the Lord GOD concerning Edom

Genesis 25:22 And the children struggled together within her; and she said, If it be so, why am I thus? And she went to enquire of the LORD.

(1)

V.13 **Thou shouldest not** have

e_____ into the g_____ of

m_____ p_____ in the

d_____ of their _____; yea,

(2)

V. 13... **thou shouldest not**

have l_____ on _____ in

t_____ a_____

the d_____ of their

c_____,

(3)

V. 13... **nor** have l_____

h_____ on their _____

s_____ in the d_____

of t_____ c_____;

(3)

V.14 **Neither shouldest thou**

have s_____ in the

c_____, to cut off those

of his that did escape;

(3)

V.14... **neither shouldest** thou have

u_____ those of

d_____

his that did remain in the d_____ of

d_____.

ARAM

PHOENICIA

ISRAEL

AMMON

Dead Sea

MOAB

JUDAH

IDUMEA

Mt. Seir

EDOM

PHILISTIA

Gulf of Aqaba

0 20 50 km

The vision of Obadiah. Thus saith
the Lord GOD concerning Edom

WARNING TO ALL HEATHEN NATIONS

Judgment Day
V.15 For the *day of the LORD* is *near* upon *all the heathen:*

as thou hast done, it shall be done unto thee: thy reward shall
return upon thine own head.

**Galatians 6:7 Be not deceived; God is not mocked: for whatsoever a man
soweth, that shall he also reap.**

Edom — of the wine from the winepress of God's wrath

V.16 For as ye have drunk upon my holy mountain, so shall all the
heathen drink continually, yea, they shall drink, and they shall
swallow down, and they shall be as though they had not been.

utterly
destroyed

heathen nations
(gentiles)

This includes America when we turn our back
on Israel as Edom did.

V.15-16
GUIDE

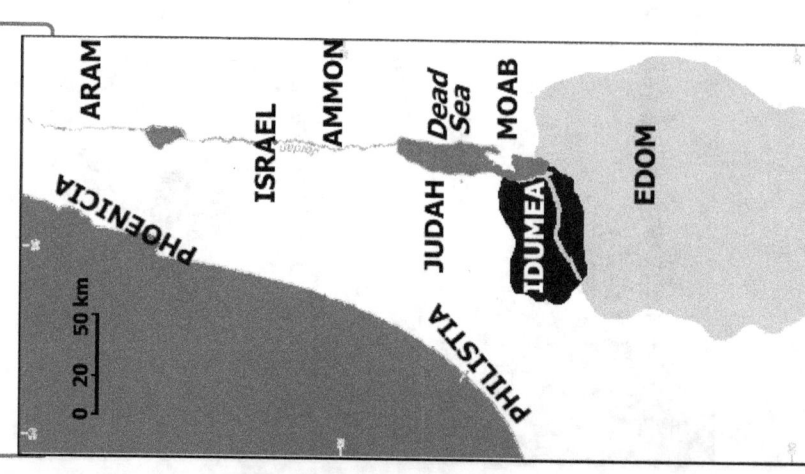

ARAM
PHOENICIA
ISRAEL
AMMON
Dead Sea
JUDAH
IDUMEA
MOAB
PHILISTIA
EDOM
Gulf of Aqaba

0   20   50 km

WARNING TO ALL HEATHEN NATIONS

V.15 For the d____ of the L____ is n____ upon a____ the h____:

as t____ hast d____, it s____ be d____ u____ t____:

thy reward shall return upon thine own head.

Galatians 6:7 Be not deceived; God is not mocked: for whatsoever a man soweth, that shall he also reap.

V.16 For as y____ have drunk upon my holy mountain, so shall all the h____ drink c____, yea, they shall drink, and they shall swallow down, and t____ shall be as though t____ h____ n____ b____.

Heathen nations that do to Jacob (Israel) shall be as Edom.
This includes America when we turn our back on Israel as Edom did.

ARAM
PHOENICIA
ISRAEL
AMMON
JUDAH
Dead Sea
MOAB
IDUMEA
EDOM
PHILISTIA
Gulf of Aqaba
0 20 50 km

About Israel

Prophecy

V.17 But upon mount Zion shall be deliverance, → *Israel*

Jerusalem

and there shall be *holiness;* and the *house of Jacob* shall possess their possessions.

Israel will possess all the Promised Land.

Israel

V.18 And the *house of Jacob* shall be a *fire,* and the *house of Joseph* a *flame,* and the *house of Esau* for *stubble,* and they shall *kindle in them,* and *fuel for the fire*

Edom

devour them; and there shall not be any remaining of the *house of Esau;* for the LORD hath spoken it.

even no more descendants

Petra

V.17-18 GUIDE

PHOENICIA
ARAM
ISRAEL
JUDAH
IDUMEA
Dead Sea
AMMON
MOAB
EDOM
Mt. Seir
PHILISTIA
Gulf of Aqaba

0 20 50 km

About Israel

V.17 But upon m_____ Z_____ shall be d_____,

and there shall be h_____; and the h_____ of

J_____ shall p_____ their p_____.

V.18 And the house of J_____ shall be a f_____, and the

house of J_____ a f_____, and the h_____ in

of E_____ for s_____, and they shall k_____

t_____, and

them; and there shall n_____ be a_____

of the house of E_____; for the L_____

d_____ s_____ it.

r_____

h_____.

V.17-18
NOTES

ARAM

AMMON

ISRAEL

PHOENICIA

Dead Sea

MOAB

JUDAH

IDUMEA

Jordan

EDOM

Mt. Seir

Gulf of Aqaba

0 20 50 km

About Israel

The children of Israel including those that were in captivity will eventually gain back their lands that the heathen nations has taken from them.

V.19 And they of the south shall possess the mount of Esau; and they of the plain the Philistines: and they shall possess the fields of Ephraim, and the fields of Samaria: and Benjamin shall possess Gilead.

V.20 And the captivity of this host of the children of Israel shall possess that of the Canaanites, even unto Zarephath; and the captivity of Jerusalem, which is in Sepharad, shall possess the cities of the south.

Genesis 12:7 And the LORD appeared unto Abram, and said, Unto thy seed will I give this land: and there builded he an altar unto the LORD, who appeared unto him.

Genesis 15:18 In the same day the LORD made a covenant with Abram, saying, Unto thy seed have I given this land, from the river of Egypt unto the great river, the river Euphrates:
Genesis 15:19 The Kenites, and the Kenizzites, and the Kadmonites,
Genesis 15:20 And the Hittites, and the Perizzites, and the Rephaims,
Genesis 15:21 And the Amorites, and the Canaanites, and the Girgashites, and the Jebusites.

V.19-20 GUIDE

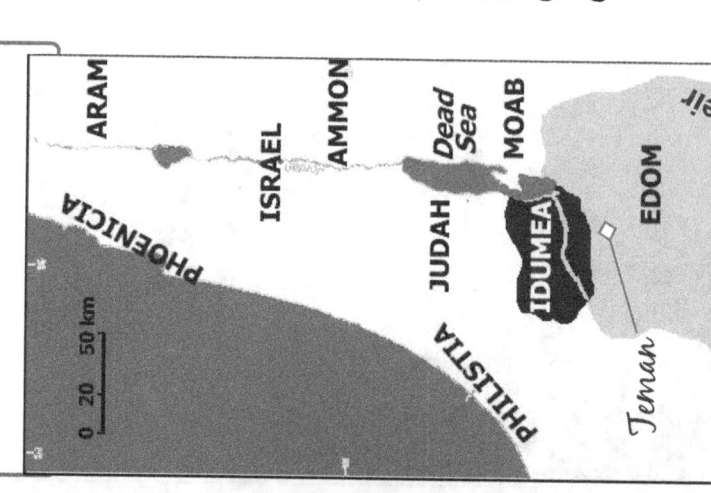

About Israel

V.19 And they of the s_____ shall possess the mount of E_____ ; and they shall
possess the f_____ of E_____ , and the fields
of S_____ : and Be_____ shall p_____
g_____ .

V.20 And the c_____ of t_____ h_____ of the
c_____ of I_____ shall possess that of the
C_____ , even unto Z_____ , which is in
c_____ of I_____ ; and the
S_____ , shall possess the c_____ of the
s_____ .

ARAM
PHOENICIA
ISRAEL
AMMON
Dead Sea
JUDAH
MOAB
IDUMEA
Mt. Seir
EDOM
PHILISTIA
Teman
Gulf of Aqaba
Bozrah
Petra

0 20   50 km

The vision of Obadiah. Thus saith
the Lord GOD concerning Edom

About Israel

1Corinthians 6:2 Do ye not
know that the saints shall
judge the world? ...

V.21 And saviours shall come up on mount Zion to judge
the mount of Esau; and the kingdom shall be the LORD's.

same warning to all heathen nations

V.21
GUIDE

Mt. Zion

Petra

ARAM

ISRAEL

AMMON

PHOENICIA

JUDAH

Dead
Sea

MOAB

IDUMEA

Mt. Seir

EDOM

PHILISTIA

Gulf of
Aqaba

0 20   50 km

The vision of Obadiah. Thus saith the Lord GOD concerning Edom

About Israel

V.21 And s_____ shall come up on
m_____ Z_____ to j_____ the
mount of E_____; and the k_____
shall be the L_____.

Valp, CC BY-SA 4.0 <https://creativecommons.org/licenses/by-sa/4.0>, via Wikimedia Commons

V.21

NOTES

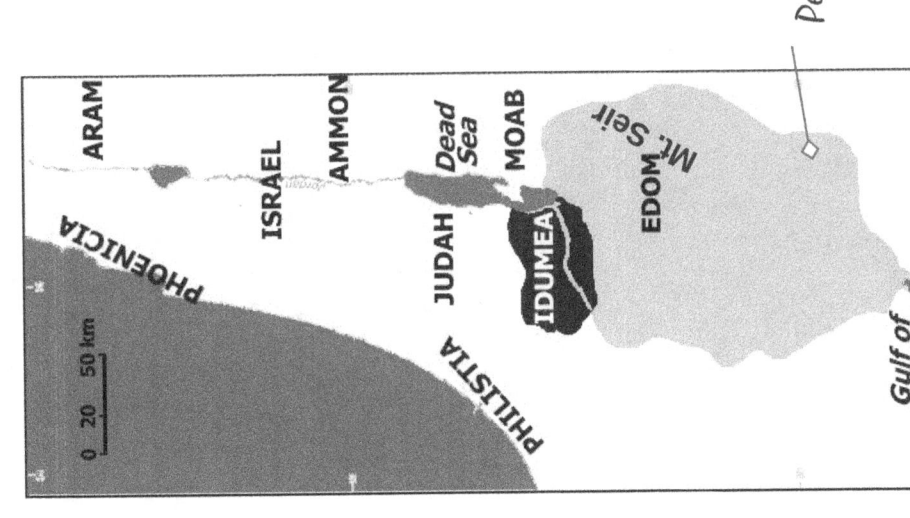

ARAM
PHOENICIA
ISRAEL
AMMON
Dead Sea
JUDAH
MOAB
IDUMEA
EDOM
Mt. Seir
PHILISTIA
Gulf of Aqaba
Petra

0 20 50 km

There is so much more!

CommonPeopleBibleStudies.com

Free Printable Lessons and Videos
Same format used in this book!
Great for individual and small group studies

Common People Bible Study Guides
Currently available on our website
- The Gospel According to John
- The Book of Ruth
- I,II,III John
- The Book of I Kings
- The Book of Obadiah

Coming Soon! Online Courses for the
Common People Bible Study Guides

Join our email list to receive new lessons as they are
published.